Economy for the Christian Home

{Cover photo: Mrs. White's front property in Vermont.}

Economy for the Christian Home

A 12 Week Challenge for Wives to Increase Charitable Giving

By Mrs. Sharon White

The Legacy of Home Press
puritanlight@gmail.com

The Legacy of Home Press
ISBN-13: 978-0692361122
ISBN-10: 069236112X
Economy for the Christian Home: A 12 Week Challenge to
Increase Charitable Giving

Author – Mrs. Sharon White

"And he saw a certain widow casting in thither two mites. And he said, of a truth I say unto you, that this poor widow hath cast in more than they all."

Luke 21: 2 - 3

Contents

Introduction

In some comfortable homes, in the early 1900's, a maid would answer the back kitchen door to a needy neighbor. Perhaps there was a sickness in the family, a husband without work, or a plea for help to buy bread for the dinner table. These requests would come in from poor people, knowing the mistress– of- the-house cared about them and did what she could to help them. She may have sent a parcel of knitted garments for poor children. She would send over a loaf of bread, meat, and fruit in a basket for those in want.

During the Depression - era, out of work men would stop at country homes asking to do some chores for a meal. The woman of the house would prepare a plate of food for them. In return, they would fix the fence, chop firewood, or whatever outdoor chores they could do. This helped ease their pride while helping her at the same time.

In the book of Ruth, we see a beautiful example of how the poor were taken care of. The law in Leviticus 19: 9 - 10 describes how landowners were to direct the reapers to leave some of the grain in the fields during harvesting. They were to leave some of the fruit in the orchards during the gathering. Once this was done, the poor would work the land, gathering the remains. In this way they were able to work and have food.

In this modern day, we need ideas and encouragement to increase charitable giving. The economy of each home should have a portion directed to giving to those in need. We can learn to make this a habit and a regular part of our lives. By managing our house - accounts using thrift, wisdom, conservation, and care, we can free up funds to alleviate some of the suffering of others.

This study is designed to be of some help. It is a 12 week challenge. Each chapter includes homework questions for discussion (for group study) or personal reflection (for private use). A financial journal has been set up in the back of the book. This is where readers can have a place to record their spending, saving, and giving during this program to see improvement and success.

If a group is using this program, here are the instructions:

1. Read the introduction before the 1st class. Each participant should also read chapter one and answer the homework questions. During the class, answers can be shared and ideas recorded.

2. Before each subsequent class, the next chapter should be read. The class can discuss and share ideas from the homework questions.

3. The Financial Journal, at the back of the book, is for each one to use privately.

1

Week One

"She ordered her household discreetly, wasted nothing, and knew no idle moment."

-Elizabeth Prentiss (a)

NOTES:

The Charity Box

Devout Jewish homes have something called a Tzedakah box. It is for charity. This is the place where money is regularly deposited in the home for later giving.

We often say to our children, "let's put some money aside for charity." But it is forgotten, or added to Mom's personal money in her purse. There is no visual image that there is a designated spot for the charitable funds.

When my children were little, and we didn't have very much money, we used a large coffee can. This was cleaned out and decorated. The children taped colored paper all around it. They decorated it with Jewish words and symbols of charity, and this is where we put our coins and such to give away.

Imagine how precious to see this type of little box, or jar, in a home. Imagine the children's joy and feelings of warmth and kindness as they contribute.

If each home is like a little sanctuary of godliness, shouldn't there be a special place for our giving?

Many of us regularly contribute a tithe (or tenth) of our income to church. Above this, there is what is called an "offering." The charity box is for this type of giving. It is a sacrificial giving, that blesses the giver.

There is always going to be a time when we struggle to put food on the table. We will struggle to find the money to pay for heat and electricity. [Of course we never use bill money to give to charity. We are responsible and pay our bills.] We are going to have rough months when just paying the rent (or mortgage) is a great feat to accomplish. But finding a way to give, as a habit, is what the charity box is for.

It can start with a penny . . . *just one penny*. Do this whenever you can, and encourage the children to find joy in depositing coins in the box as well. This habit of giving, despite economic trouble, will help develop a habit of saving.

They both work together - giving and saving, even just a tiny amount. This develops discipline which will sharpen and strengthen our money management skills. To take care of one's own family and bless others at the same time is to be an excellent steward of the funds placed into our hands. This is doing the Lord's work. It can all start with a charity box in the home.

Week One - Discussion Questions

1)

"And now abideth faith, hope, charity, these three; but the greatest of these is charity." –

I Corinthians 13:13

Define "faith."

Define "hope."

Define "charity."

Why would charity be the greatest?

2)

Who are the poor and how do we find them?

3)

Name places where we can donate money. How do we know if a charity is reputable?

Challenge: Buy or make your own charity box. What does your family think about it? In what ways can you involve them?

2

Week Two

"Herman and Minnie were to knit all the way to school, for the walk was long. Each carried a little basket on the arm, to hold the ball of yarn."

- Elizabeth Prentiss (b)

NOTES:

Feeding Others

There is something called, "The Deacon's Fund" in most churches. This is for designated financial contributions to help the poor in a congregation. Some may need help with their heat bill one month. Another might be in crisis and need an electric bill paid. Mostly, it is used to help provide food for the hungry.

In one Massachusetts church I attended, the Deacon's wives were in charge of feeding those in need. They would organize food baskets at Thanksgiving and Christmas. They would find out who was having a baby, or recovering from surgery, and make calls for volunteers to provide hot meals for a few days to help those families in need.

There are food pantries in just about every town, or community. Some are government agencies, others are run by churches. Food drives are always sponsored by schools and local businesses. While we can certainly drop off canned goods when these are requested, we can also bring in donations ourselves to our favorite places.

One year, the children and I had some extra money. We did our regular grocery shopping, but we also shopped for the food pantry. We bought things we wanted to eat ourselves - things that were treats - like cake mix, name brand soups, and staple items like vegetable oil for baking. When we got home, the children separated the charity items from our own groceries and put ours away. We then packed a large box full of groceries. Inside we included an anonymous note for the recipient, wishing them a good day. This was then taken to a small food pantry which was run by a group of elderly volunteers who we loved. They were the sweetest people. We did this a few times and the children loved it. We also knew that the recipient would be blessed and eat well that week.

Obviously we are not always able to give large amounts of food or money, but that should not stop us from making an effort. If all we have that month is $10 to spare, consider giving it to your church's Deacon's fund where it will be added to other funds and greatly bless someone in need.

Week Two - Discussion Questions

1)

"And the King shall answer and say unto them, Verily I say unto you, Inasmuch as ye have done it unto one of the least of these my brethren, ye have done it unto me." –

Matthew 25:40

What does this verse mean to you?

2)

Is there a Deacon's fund in your church? How does it work? In what ways can you help?

3)

Where is your local food pantry? Are there ways you can help? (Example: Volunteering or donating food.)

Challenge: This week gather up some food to donate to a food pantry. Try your very best to come up with a few dollars to contribute to your church's Deacon's fund

3

Week Three

"We call ourselves poor, and make a great time about it, but just fancy living upon four hundred dollars a year, as the Western Missionary does."

- Elizabeth Prentiss (c)

NOTES:

Finding Good Deed Money

My husband has often said to me, "Do we have any money left in the fund?" He is talking about our "Good Deed Money." He may have heard of someone in crisis at work, or it is time to visit an elderly, lonely neighbor who needs groceries to cheer him along the way.

Now I have to say, we have spent most of our married life living in borderline poverty in the eyes of society and, other than some frightening years of "want," we have been able to put aside something to give to those in need. Anything from pennies, to dollars, to hundreds is plenty to do one little helpful thing in the world around us. A good deed, an act of giving, can cost very little, but it blesses both the recipient and the giver! It is most wonderful when it is done anonymously.

The adventure in giving is finding the money with which to share. Over the past few months I've been staying home almost constantly. Someone else has been doing my errands combined with their own trips, so that has saved us gas money. We budget a certain amount each week for gas, but I noticed that we never spend the entire amount. So this "extra" money has been handed over to my husband to save for needs that come up.

Most of us can also find change all over the house when we do some deep cleaning. Money is in couch cushions, the laundry, behind bureaus, and even in the recycling of cans and bottles! This change can go into a charity box and be used for good deeds.

It is essential that we are good stewards of the money God puts into our hands. When we scrimp and save money to give to charity, we have to be sure the need is genuine. It is not okay to blindly give -just to give. This is where prayer comes in, and making certain that before we hand over money for those good deeds, we have complete peace in our hearts and minds.

Week Three - Discussion Questions

1)

".. A prudent wife is from the Lord." –

Proverbs 19:14

Define "prudent."

In what ways can we be prudent?

How is this a blessing to your husband?

2)

In what ways can you use spare change to do good deeds?

3)

What are you able to "give up" each week to free up money for those in need?

Challenge: Find some spare money around the house this week. Use it for a charitable purpose.

4

Week Four

"How a woman handles something as impermanent and worldly as money reveals how well she can be trusted with great spiritual resources."

- Elizabeth Rice Handford (d)

NOTES:

A Little Bit Cold and Other Ways to Save Money

In my childhood home, New England winters by the ocean were bitterly cold. We children would always wear a robe or sweater in the house. We had oil heat but it was carefully conserved to make it affordable for my parents. Dad would have a fire in the fireplace on weekends or some evenings when he was home from work. This helped warm us up and keep us cheerful.

People today are used to comfort and don't realize what it means to be frugal with their money. We come from great Pioneer stock who couldn't even fathom the riches and modern conveniences we have today. We can learn to do with a little less so that money is freed up for savings.

Obviously, we cannot give away all our extra money. We have to slowly, over time, build up some savings to provide for the needs of our family. Many of us struggle to pay our property taxes each year. We may struggle to pay for our winter heat. This is where a habit of consistent saving throughout the year will help us get through the difficult times.

We must also be an example of prudence to our children. Recently, I told the children about this movie I wanted to buy.

When I found out the price, I was shocked. It was seriously overpriced. One of the children said that since I wanted it so much, he would buy it for me. This is where we explain "supply and demand" and how it is not wise to buy something that is frivolously priced. We have to go without that wanted item and refuse to waste our hard earned money. Our spending must be bathed in common sense and wisdom. We will not waste our money. We must carefully use it in the right way.

This foundational thinking will greatly help in our savings. Around the house, there are many ways to save. I did an experiment with the clothes dryer for a couple of months. In the summer I would hang towels on the clothesline or on backs of chairs in the winter. They take too long in the dryer and I wanted to keep the electric bill low. When I noticed this was only saving me $10 a month, I was tempted to just stop wasting my time by air drying them, and just use the dryer. But this little effort is not that difficult and the $10 savings will add up to $120 at the end of the year! $120 is a large amount to save when you think about it in the long term.

Here in Vermont it is easy to go without air conditioning in the summertime. We have some very hot days where it is tempting, but it is not worth the high electric bill! Thinking about history and what it must have been like before electricity was common will help ease our feeling of deprivation. Families who lived in the cities of New England were very hot, and

Economy for the Christian Home

wanted to escape, in the summer, to the country and beaches for relief. There is a coolness to the air and we can adjust to going without the air conditioning. However, in hotter climates, like California and Alabama, I could not imagine living without the necessity of air conditioning! We just have to find ways to save that make sense in the area in which we live.

Saving money on groceries is always a challenge. Don't be fooled by your grocer's receipt with the total in bold print of "how much you saved." It is a modern - day marketing ploy. The truth is, you save money when you don't spend it. In the case of grocery shopping, you would have a budgeted amount for the week. Any amount of cash you have left from that budget is what you actually "saved." This goes for any budgeted amount you have in all spending categories. Put aside even $5 in each category by working hard at frugality, conservation, and portion control and you should have a nice amount to save each month.

NOTES:

Week Four - Discussion Questions

1)

"The soul of the sluggard desireth, and hath nothing: but the soul of the diligent shall be made fat." –

Proverbs 13:4

In what ways can this verse apply to saving money in the home?

2)

What is the difference between being "idle" and genuine "rest"? In what ways can "idleness" cause us to waste time and money?

3)

How can you involve your family is saving money?

Challenge: Do four things this week to cut back on expenses.

5

Week Five

"For only seven pennies, you can buy a miniature comic-book style tract guaranteed to be read."

- Mrs. Delores Elaine Bius (e)

NOTES:

When Money Comes In

There are always some kind of fundraisers happening at the stores and malls. These are usually for some well - known organization. Many of us are asked if we'd like to donate as our purchases are being rung up. Almost as an afterthought we would say, yes, and then go about our life. While it is certainly good to give in these situations, it is even better to make it part of a routine - plan to give.

Perhaps we could have a little compartment in our purse for charity. If we write down the amount we start out with (even if it is just 5 - one dollar bills a week), then jot down the reason and amount of giving, we can keep track. This is something we can look over, privately, and reflect.

It can become a habit of *living to give*, rather than an afterthought which is usually forgotten.

All churches have donation envelopes. You can request several at a time (or an entire box with 52 - one for each week of the year), and bring it home with you. This will become a tool of giving. Each week you can prepare the envelope while doing your bills. You may have had a windfall and could put in a large sum of money. Some weeks you may have more to give than others, but even if only a dollar is placed in an envelope you are going to be blessed because giving becomes a joyous habit that will fill your heart with peace. Pray over that money that it will be used to bless someone.

If you have a "charity box," which involves the whole family, have someone count the coins on a weekly or monthly basis and then discuss and pray together about where the money should be given. Including the children in this helps set a habit of faith in prayer and a heart for the less fortunate.

Consider writing down how much is given and where it was given. Over the course of a year you will want to look at this journal. You will want to remember that the money placed into your charge is being used for eternal purposes.

Week Five - Discussion Questions

1)

"And this stone, which I have set for a pillar, shall be God's house: and of all that thou shalt give me I will surely give the tenth unto thee." –

Genesis 28:22

This is Jacob's promise. How much discipline will it require?

What does this verse mean to you?

2)

In what ways can you organize your giving to make it a habit?

3)

If you only had $1 to give away, what would you do with it?
What if you had $100 to give away?

Challenge: Write down where you gave your donations this
week. Look over the financial journal (in the back of this book)
and try to increase the amount you are giving to "charity."
(Pennies count just as much as dollars. Any increase is a
success.)

6

Week Six

"You are richer than you think. No matter how limited your resources. When you give a dollar, the Lord will not only double its purchasing power and repay you, but you are also depositing money in your heavenly savings account."

- Mrs. Delores Elaine Bius (f)

NOTES:

Prayer Directed Giving

Sometimes we will feel a conviction which guides us in our giving to others. I remember one year, I realized my father didn't have a blender. I think his had broken at some point. So I saved up and bought him one, planning to give it to him on Father's day. Well, it was put aside in May. As the weeks went by Dad got very sick. He had to have a procedure done on his throat making it almost impossible to eat. He was so hungry but in great pain. When Mother told this to me, I said, "Well, I have a blender for Dad. I was saving it for Father's day, but I will give it to him now. I also have a new can of protein powder that hasn't been opened. I will send these down to you." They were both shocked. How could this great need be given so quickly? This is an example of prayer directed giving. The Lord put these things into place in His own time. Mom and Dad prayed for help and God had the blender and shake - mix all ready to go! It was such a shock and a blessing to us all!

Another instance of this type of giving happened many years ago, starting on a Sunday morning. I gathered the children and we got ready for church. I had some money we had put aside, planning to give to the church as a special offering. I put this in my purse. But when I got there, and the offering plate came around, I could not hand over the money. I had this strong conviction that I was not to give. This baffled me. I knew I had a wonderful church. I knew the work they were doing was honorable and right. So why the strong feeling not to give? I did not understand.

My husband was not at church with me that day. So when I got home, I told him what had happened. "Something must be going on," he said. "Just put the money aside and we will keep adding to it."

This went on for months. We were praying about where the money was needed. We continued about our daily lives, saving for, and adding to, that special fund.

One day I was on the phone with the Grandparents. They had traveled out of state and were staying near my Aunt. They had been there for a few months. There had been a fire at my Aunt's house and she was in the hospital. Living arrangements were made to move her into a temporary trailer beside her home while the rebuilding took place. The Grandparents were there to help, but their health was suffering at the same time. My husband and I suddenly knew what all that money had been for. On the telephone, Grandmother was her usual cheerful self, but told me they were having a rough time with all the added expenses of being away from home. They were worried about their bills and such. I told her, "Well, we have some money we have been saving for a long time. And we prayed about it. We feel that this money is for you and

Economy for the Christian Home

Grandpa." I heard her telling her husband, who was sitting nearby. I could hear him crying. I didn't want them to wonder or worry anymore so I told her the amount. "We have $700 for you." I heard Grandpa's cracked, shaking voice cry out, through tears, "Oh, Thank God!" It broke my heart.

My husband and I couldn't help but cry at this miracle. While this is a rare case, and doesn't often happen, it is an example of prayer directed giving. Others around us pray for help, but don't always share their burden with others. God then lays it on the hearts of His people to help. When we listen, sometimes patiently waiting for the revealed time, we are all blessed by the result.

Economy for the Christian Home

NOTES:

Week Six -Discussion Questions

1)

". . . The effectual fervent prayer of a righteous man availeth much." –

James 5:16

Define "fervent."

Define "righteous."

How can this kind of praying help you?

2)

How will praying over your donation money help? In what ways can we notice the needs of others around us?

3)

Have you ever felt led by the Lord, in prayer, to give money?
What happened?

Challenge: Write down an answer to prayer that happened in
your life. This week pray for the Lord to lead you to help
someone in need.

7

Week Seven

"I shall have more than a hundred dollars to give away each year, as long as I live! How perfectly delightful. I can hardly conceive of anything that could give me so much pleasure!"

- Elizabeth Prentiss (g)

NOTES:

New England Thrift

There is a Yankee mentality here in rural New England. We make do, wear things out, and are practical about our possessions. We wouldn't dream of buying a new, upgraded refrigerator if the one we had still worked. We wouldn't replace kitchen flooring if there was still life in our current floor. We would repair and clean things up and make them last as long as possible. This is a frugal, thrifty life. It is practical and careful.

It is a common thing to see simple duct tape on broken items around a thrifty home. This makes them last longer so money is conserved. We decorate and clean and make a humble home look nice and pleasant despite the Yankee repairs. It adds charm to a home and helps build up the savings account.

Money should not be wasted on frivolous items. One of the problems of this culture is that we are constantly encouraged to buy new things. It has become normal to go to the grocery store (or local drug store) and find movies for sale, or gift items that we pick up for ourselves and our children. It used to be that those luxuries were only bought for a birthday or holiday. Gifts were given once or twice a year, not every single week, or every single time the family goes out.

As a boy in the 1940's, my father would walk into a country store with Grandpa. He would see all the wonderful, exciting things and he would look at them while Grandpa shopped for necessities. He would not have even thought of asking for a dime to buy something. It would not have entered his mind to say, "Can you buy me some candy?" In those days children knew the value of money and knew they had to work to earn the extras. Today's culture is so different, but we can make a change in our own families.

An attitude of New England Thrift and Yankee Ingenuity is what will help us build up savings in our own homes. It will help us be practical and careful. This will help us in our giving and in our management of the money God gives us.

Week Seven - Discussion Questions

1)

"Ye have sown much, and bring in little; ye eat, but ye have not enough; ye drink, but ye are not filled with drink; ye clothe you, but there is none warm; and he that earneth wages earneth wages to put it into a bag with holes. Thus saith the Lord of hosts; Consider your ways." –

Haggai 1:6 –7

Many never seem to have enough money. They may be working hard, but the money goes too fast. How does this passage from the Bible relate to homes of today?

2)

In what ways were your Grandparents thrifty?

3)

Name two thrifty ideas unique to your area of the country.

Challenge: Do one new thing to "make do" and "go without" this week in order to help your household be more frugal.

8

Week Eight

"Housekeeping was commenced on a very modest scale . . . She was a splendid manageress, and by means of rigid economies quite a substantial amount was saved toward the support and education of the first student. . .

The chief difficulty with regard to money in those days was to make 'both ends meet.' We never had enough left over to 'tie a bow and ends.' But I see now that this was God's way of preparing us to sympathize with and help poor pastors in the years which were to come."

- The Life of Susannah Spurgeon (Wife of C.H. Spurgeon) (h)

NOTES:

Do Not Borrow

It should be our life goal to avoid borrowing money. In this culture it is common to use credit cards for shopping, food, or to pay bills. It became an expected convenience and has gained public favor in the eyes of a nation who used to have great pride in avoiding the burden of debt.

When we are in the stores, we should only spend what we have available. Spending borrowed money means we are contributing to the business of debt that has ruined many homes across the land. Most people cannot pay their balance in full each month. They are then paying extra for everything they buy. This makes the credit companies rich and powerful.

We need to find ways to live within the income God has provided us with. By avoiding debt, interest charges, and monthly debt payments, we will free up money for savings and giving. We will live in peace rather than in dread. We will be free instead of slaves to the lender.

One of my girls recently told me she spent several hundred dollars on Christmas gifts. She felt bad, that perhaps she had spent too much money. While many of us have times of overspending, I told her she had a reason to be proud of herself. "How many people paid cash for their gifts this year and didn't use credit?" I asked her. "You spent hard earned cash for those gifts. You didn't borrow it. You will have peace about it in a couple of weeks when most others will have feelings of remorse and despair when they get their credit card bills." I know she will easily earn back that money in a short time and be back on track. But most of all, she won't be paying off debts as she is trying to earn back her savings!

There is a sense of accomplishment and joy when we spend only what we earn. In these times, it is a great feat to not borrow money. We should make it our daily aim to find creative ways to avoid debt.

Week Eight - Discussion Questions

1)

"The rich ruleth over the poor, and the borrower is servant to the lender.." –

Proverbs 22:7

In what cases do the rich rule over the poor?

How is a borrower the lender's servant?

2)

How will credit card debt make it hard for you to give and save?

3)

How does living simply and humbly help us sympathize with those living in poverty?

Challenge: Set up a budget for the week in a way that you will live below your income. You may have to give up some things in order to accomplish this.

9

Week Nine

"There were times when the devoted couple abstained from almost necessary things in order to have money to help on the work."

- The Life of Susanna Spurgeon (Wife of C.H. Spurgeon) (i)

NOTES:

Earning to Give

Many of us find ways to come up with extra spending money. We might want a treat or we may want to save up for some event. In these cases we work a little harder to come up with those needed funds. At other times, we could use those same techniques to earn extra money to give away.

Yard sales are common ways to earn money. If you have one or two of these in the summertime, consider taking all or part of that money and giving it to charity.

There are consignment shops and second hand stores where we can sell things we no longer need for cash. We can also sell used books and movies online for a return of a few cents to a few dollars. This can be added to a charity box for later giving.

Some are creative and can spend time with the family making things like woodwork, embroidery, clothing, and jewelry. The little side business could be all for charity or a set portion (such as half) could be put in the charity box. You may want to simply make things to give away without selling them. These could be items like crocheted baby blankets for new mothers at the local hospital. These could be added to the "welcome basket" they receive as they are recovering. A note could be attached with a kind word and the name of your "anonymous" organization.

I once read about some children who started doing good deeds. When an elderly relative was not at home, they raked her yard. On another day, they bought a few little groceries, put them in a box and left them on the front porch of a needy family. They rang the doorbell and then ran before they could be seen. Each time they did a kind deed for someone else; they left a little note and signed it "anonymous." We can use our own labor and extra money to secretly bless others. This makes it so much fun!

This industry in the home gives more meaning to life and keeps us busy. It is a blessing and an incredible example to our children. It also warms the heart to know that our labor is helping the needy.

Week Nine - Discussion Questions

1)

"Then saith he unto his disciples, The harvest truly is plenteous, but the labourers are few." –

Matthew 9:37

What is "the harvest" referred to in this verse?

Who are "the labourers?" Why are there so few of them?

2)

In what ways can we be productive at home that would earn money for charity?

3)

What fun ways can your family help others anonymously?

Challenge: Work on learning a new skill this week (such as painting, knitting, gourmet cooking, etc.) that you can use to bless others.

10

Week Ten

"Blessed is he that considereth the poor: the Lord will deliver him in time of trouble." - Psalm 41:1

NOTES:

The Prayer Chain

One of the main ways we find out about a need is through the church's prayer chain. This is when you receive a phone call for current prayers within the congregation. I would get calls every few days - someone was in the hospital, or someone had fallen, or there was a death in a family, etc. The call was brief. I would stop whatever I was doing. Then, after I hung up, I would pray while getting back to my housework. Others would receive prayer alerts through email. This was a wonderful way to be aware of the needs of fellow church members. These were people you knew, people you saw every week in the local church. They were the church family.

Early last year, my parents (who lived with me at the time, in an in-law apartment in my house) were in great need of prayer. Dad had been rushed to the hospital because he had fallen on the ice, causing trauma to his head. While he and Mother were in the emergency room, I was on the phone calling their Pastor. This started a prayer chain for them. Over the next several days, while Dad was in the hospital, I kept in touch with their Pastor with prayer requests and updates on his condition. Church members came to the hospital to visit. Everyone prayed. When Dad was finally able to come home to continue his recovery, we were told they would receive a hot dinner each night for a week from volunteers in the church. This was an incredible blessing. Many people will say, "Please let me know if there is anything I can do." Or they may say, "Do you need anything?" Most of us would say, "No thank you. I am fine." We don't want to ask. We don't want to bother anyone. But when the church has a program in place, where they automatically come to the aid of those in crisis, without asking, this is an incredible answer to silent prayers.

Each night, around 5 p.m., a car would pull into the driveway with dinner. It was January. Our Vermont winters are icy and bitter. We were so grateful for those who came by each night despite the cold. I remember one person, in particular. I was sitting in the living room, visiting with my parents, when a car pulled in. Mother and I went to the kitchen door. The woman said, "Hello, I am Mrs. Jones from the Church. I brought your dinner." She then stepped in, holding a rectangular shaped, insulated container. Inside were two aluminum foil pans. She left them on the counter and then said, "God bless you," as she walked back out the door. She had her young children with her. They looked so excited to be a part of this!

The dinner contained a creamed chicken and vegetable dish topped with cracker crumbs. The other pan held four raspberry oat bars. My Mother was delighted. Her own health was failing. Worrying about Dad and taking care of him was draining. Here was a hot, nutritious dinner which came from a member of her own church. She didn't have to worry about shopping, cooking, or cleaning the mess. It was wonderful!

Economy for the Christian Home

Week Ten - Discussion Questions

1)

"And when Jesus was come into Peter's house, he saw his wife's mother laid, and sick of a fever. And he touched her hand, and the fever left her: and she arose, and ministered unto them." –

Matthew 8:14 – 15

When the Mother was healed, why do you think she got up and ministered to them?

When we are visited by the Lord's people during a sickness, could this have a similar affect on us? Would it help to cheer us so that we get well sooner?

2)

Does your church have a prayer chain? How can you get involved?

3)

What are good, nutritious meal ideas to provide a hot dinner to share with someone in crisis?

Challenge: This week, visit or write to someone who is alone, ill, or hospitalized. Encourage them in some way.

11

Week Eleven

"She stretcheth out her hand to the poor; yea, she reacheth forth her hands to the needy."

- Proverbs 31:20

NOTES:

Living in Reduced Circumstances

"For the poor shall never cease out of the land: therefore I command thee, saying, Thou shalt open thine hand wide unto thy brother, to thy poor, and to thy needy, in thy land." – Deuteronomy 15:11

Most of us will have a time when we are in great need of charity. The economy has its ups and downs. Our personal lives also go through times of trial, want, and suffering. Those who have received a charitable gift during a rough time understand how truly blessed it is to give to those in need.

Several years ago, during a major oil crisis, gas prices rose to over $4.50 a gallon here in rural Vermont. This caused food prices to skyrocket, partly due to the cost of fuel for the freight trucks who were delivering inventory to all the supermarkets.

Many could not afford to drive to work and had to find ways to carpool, walk, or find some other form of transportation. I remember having to give up going to church and limiting youth group events for my (then) teenage children. It was shocking to realize we couldn't afford the gas to drive to church!

One of the hardest things during this time was having just enough food to feed one's family with little or nothing left over to share with a guest. Many did not entertain at home. Having company was rare and difficult. Offering just a cup of tea to a guest when one wanted to offer cake or pie was depressing!

Nobody wants to live in want or hunger. Nobody wants to feel like buying sugar to bake cookies would be a financial burden when the family needed more nutritious foods like vegetables or meat.

Food pantries in our county were suddenly full of the more affluent in our area. We were told that many could not afford to buy food and pay basic living expenses at the same time. One large church in our area was open on a daily basis and gave out emergency food boxes which were expected to last a family, or individual, for a couple of days. We were seeing both homeless and middle class in the same breadlines. Nobody wanted to be there. Nobody wanted to need charity, but the economy forced many to seek help just to eat.

Another church in our area had a monthly potluck supper offered right after the morning service. Almost everyone brought hot food, desserts, salads, bread and treats to share with each other. This way each family could contribute what they could and enjoy a nice big meal without feeling like they were getting a handout. This same church also provides a large spread of refreshments in the dining room after every Sunday service. Most of the food is brought in by members of the congregation and is a lovely way to comfort one another with both food and fellowship.

There were certain days of the week where local supermarkets would provide display tables with food samples. Children of customers were also given a cookie from the bakery or a piece of cheese from the deli. This made grocery shopping, on limited funds, a special outing and a way to gratefully enjoy a special treat. It benefited the stores as well since they were able to offer new foods, and have a nice way to encourage customers to shop.

Today, times are better. Gas prices have dropped to around $2.88 in our area. This is the lowest I have seen it here since before the oil crisis hit our nation. Yet, there will always be someone, or some family, struggling through a time of poverty, a time of "reduced circumstances." These are the people on a financial adventure who will overcome the difficulties with prayer, faith, hard work, and the blessing of a good church family.

NOTES:

Week Eleven - Discussion Questions

1)

"If I take the wings of the morning, and dwell in the uttermost parts of the sea; Even there shall thy hand lead me, and thy right hand shall hold me." –

Psalm 139:9 – 10

Is this verse a beautiful description of the Lord being with us no matter where we are?

In what times of trouble can this comfort us?

2)

Have you ever suffered through a financial trial? What did others do that was helpful?

Economy for the Christian Home

3)

How can you show hospitality to guests when you have limited resources?

Challenge: Say a prayer this week for those in your church who are suffering financially. Talk to church leaders to see if there is one thing you can do to help.

12

Week Twelve

"She looketh well to the ways of her household, and eateth not the bread of idleness."

-Proverbs 31:27

NOTES:

Treasures in the House

I once read that Mrs. John R. Rice (the wife of a famous evangelist, and the mother of six children) had her house full of ministry work. The back room held inventory stock of her husband's books. The dining room was buzzing with activity with the addressing and mailing of her husband's Christian newspaper. Guests came to stay all the time to help with the work. She fed the helpers along with her own family. She also sewed clothes for herself and children. She decorated the home, and made curtains. She was a great blessing to many in her homemaking and ministry work. She was a noble helper to her husband in his great work for the Lord.

Few of us are so blessed to do a united work such as was done by the Rice family. In this modern society we are often swept up with the rest of the culture in doing our own thing or spending our money on "upgrades" and personal entertainment. Because of this, we are missing out on the real joy in living. Our treasures are to be in heaven. We ought to have things that would bless others - such as food to share and Christian literature. This is where having "treasures in the house" would make our own homes like the central station of missionary work!

We should consider having a supply of Bibles, tracts, spiritual books, and good food to share with others when opportunities arise. These are the treasures in our homes.

When my fifth child was 2 years old, he had some health problems. Every few months I would have to take him into a large hospital in the city of Boston for check-ups. A young couple always went with me as my guide. We would take the subway. I would hold that baby and our things and we would be sitting at the dark, underground station, waiting for the subway. Almost every single time a person would come up to me asking for money or food. I didn't have much, but I always had pocket Bibles in my bag to give away. Most people would sneer and walk away. But some were hungry for spiritual warmth and would gladly take one.

The children and I also had a supply of little tracts. These were like small folded brochures with the gospel message. I would put one in with my bills to be mailed out. The children would leave some at the park, on cars in lots, or hand them out to those who were receptive.

What makes this so precious is that the entire family is a part of this missionary work. The home is the station for spreading forth the gospel, comforting souls, and leading them to the peace that passeth all understanding. This is where a portion of our money should be invested.

Week Twelve - Discussion Questions

1)

"How beautiful upon the mountains are the feet of him that bringeth good tidings, that publisheth peace; that bringeth good tidings of good, that publisheth salvation; that saith unto Zion, Thy God reigneth!" –

Isaiah 52:7

Can you name three ways we can do what this verse says?

Who is blessed by this? (Example: Seekers, the messenger, etc.)

2)

What Christian literature would you stock up on to give away?

3)

How can you involve your family in Christian outreach?

Challenge: This week, buy some type of literature (a tract, Bible, inspiring book, etc.) and give it away.

"The heart of her husband doth safely trust in her, so that he shall have no need of spoil."

Proverbs 31:11

Economy for the Christian Home

Economy for the Christian Home

Appendix

Economy for the Christian Home

Financial Journal

(Confidential)

"House Account"

The house account is money used to pay for groceries, clothing, gasoline, charity, and other miscellaneous items. For our purposes, it is any money other than what we use for our bills. However, for those who feel more comfortable including all bills and expenses, extra space has been provided for your convenience.

Each week we will write down the amount used in different categories. The goal is to see the savings and giving columns increase in the beginning, and then remain steady through the rest of the 12 week challenge.

Use a notebook to write down your daily spending. Don't forget cash, checks, and debit card purchases. At the end of the week, record your totals here.

Week One   Date _____

Grocery $ _____

Gasoline / Transportation $ _____

Clothing $ _____

Savings $ _____

Charity $ _____

Other $ _____

_____ $ _____

_____ $ _____

_____ $ _____

_____ $ _____

_____ $ _____

Notes:

Economy for the Christian Home

Week Two   Date _____

Grocery $ _____

Gasoline / Transportation $ _____

Clothing $ _____

Savings $ _____

Charity $ _____

Other $ _____

_____ $ _____

_____ $ _____

_____ $ _____

_____ $ _____

_____ $ _____

Notes

Economy for the Christian Home

Week Three   Date _____

Grocery $ _____

Gasoline / Transportation $ _____

Clothing $ _____

Savings $ _____

Charity $ _____

Other $ _____

_____ $ _____

_____ $ _____

_____ $ _____

_____ $ _____

_____ $ _____

Notes

Week Four   Date _____

Grocery $ _____

Gasoline / Transportation $ _____

Clothing $ _____

Savings $ _____

Charity $ _____

Other $ _____

_____ $ _____

_____ $ _____

_____ $ _____

_____ $ _____

_____ $ _____

Notes

Economy for the Christian Home

Week Five   Date _____

Grocery $ _____

Gasoline / Transportation $ _____

Clothing $ _____

Savings $ _____

Charity $ _____

Other $ _____

_____ $ _____

_____ $ _____

_____ $ _____

_____ $ _____

_____ $ _____

Notes

Week Six   Date _____

Grocery $ _____

Gasoline / Transportation $ _____

Clothing $ _____

Savings $ _____

Charity $ _____

Other $ _____

_____ $ _____

_____ $ _____

_____ $ _____

_____ $ _____

_____ $ _____

Notes

Economy for the Christian Home

Week Seven   Date _____

Grocery $ _____

Gasoline / Transportation $ _____

Clothing $ _____

Savings $ _____

Charity $ _____

Other $ _____

_____ $ _____

_____ $ _____

_____ $ _____

_____ $ _____

_____ $ _____

Notes

Week Eight   Date _____

Grocery $ _____

Gasoline / Transportation $ _____

Clothing $ _____

Savings $ _____

Charity $ _____

Other $ _____

_____ $ _____

_____ $ _____

_____ $ _____

_____ $ _____

_____ $ _____

Notes

Economy for the Christian Home

Week Nine   Date _____

Grocery $ _____

Gasoline / Transportation $ _____

Clothing $ _____

Savings $ _____

Charity $ _____

Other $ _____

_____ $ _____

_____ $ _____

_____ $ _____

_____ $ _____

_____ $ _____

Notes

Week Ten   Date _____

Grocery $ _____

Gasoline / Transportation $ _____

Clothing $ _____

Savings $ _____

Charity $ _____

Other $ _____

_____ $ _____

_____ $ _____

_____ $ _____

_____ $ _____

_____ $ _____

Notes

Economy for the Christian Home

Week Eleven   Date _____

Grocery $ _____

Gasoline / Transportation $ _____

Clothing $ _____

Savings $ _____

Charity $ _____

Other $ _____

_____ $ _____

_____ $ _____

_____ $ _____

_____ $ _____

_____ $ _____

Notes

Week Twelve   Date _____

Grocery $ _____

Gasoline / Transportation $ _____

Clothing $ _____

Savings $ _____

Charity $ _____

Other $ _____

_____ $ _____

_____ $ _____

_____ $ _____

_____ $ _____

_____ $ _____

Notes

Final Account   Date _____

12 Weeks of Total Saved $ _____

12 Weeks of Total Charity Given $ _____

Notes:

Bibliography of Quotes

(a)

"The Little Preacher" (1800's) by Elizabeth Prentiss, page 13.

(b)

"The Little Preacher" (1800's) by Elizabeth Prentiss, page 23.

(c)

"Aunt Jane's Hero" (1800's) by Elizabeth Prentiss, page136.

(d)

"How to Get your Money's Worth. . Without Being Nasty" ("The Joyful Woman Magazine," May 1984.) by Elizabeth Rice Handford, page 5.

(e)

"Never Underestimate the Power of a Dollar" ("The Joyful Woman Magazine," May 1982.) by Mrs. Delores Elaine Bius, page 6.

(f)

"Never Underestimate the Power of a Dollar" ("The Joyful Woman Magazine," May 1982.) by Mrs. Delores Elaine Bius, page 6.

(g)

"Stepping Heavenward" (1800's) by Elizabeth Prentiss, page 205.

(h)

"The Life of Susannah Spurgeon" (1903) by Charles Ray, page 157.

(i)

"The Life of Susannah Spurgeon" (1903) by Charlest Ray, page 157.

Books by Mrs. White

Mother's Faith

For the Love of Christian Homemaking

Early Morning Revival Challenge

Mother's Book of Home Economics

Living on His Income

Old Fashioned Motherhood

Economy for the Christian Home

About the Author

Mrs. White is a housewife of more than a quarter of a century, a beloved mother of five children, and grandmother of four. She is the granddaughter of revival preacher, LD Murphy. She lives in an 1800's house in rural Vermont.

For more information or to find Mrs. White's books, please visit:

The Legacy of Home Press

http://thelegacyofhomepress.blogspot.com

Also see Mrs. White's blog:

http://thelegacyofhome.blogspot.com